THERE ARE MORE CAMERAS THAN PICKET SIGNS

How Outrage
Became Optics and
Protests Became Performances

Jereme Silltech

ISBN: 978-1-964026-13-8 (paperback)
ISBN: 978-1-964026-14-5 (ebook)

THERE ARE MORE CAMERAS THAN PICKET SIGNS:
How Outrage Became Optics and Protests Became Performances

MH

MICHTER HOUSE
PUBLISHING
an imprint of
Rope Swing Publishing

www.ropeswingpublishing.com

To The Voices Behind True Change

INTRODUCTION

Trendy, but Not Always on Point.

This book started as a question I couldn't shake: When did activism become a performance? Watching any news outlet, spanning all political lines, I notice the same theme... activism for headlines.

Somewhere along the way, we traded picket signs and work behind the scenes for perfectly posed protest selfies or news coverage. We started measuring impact by engagement. We got loud, but not always clear. We got visible, but not always effective. We got trendy, but not always on point.

I'm not here to scold or shame anyone. I've been part of the problem, too. I've scrolled and read just about every outrage post and news story I could find. I've understood posting conviction into a caption and wondered why it all felt so... hollow.

This isn't an anti-tech rant or a call to unplug and disappear into the woods. I like Wi-Fi and a good meme, but I also like truth and justice. I think it's time we talked about what happens when cameras outnumber picket signs, as we have started performing our values instead of living them.

I guess I'm writing this more as part cultural critique, part personal reflection, and part rally cry. It's about the difference between optics and action. It's about who gets heard, who gets filmed, and who gets erased. It's about reclaiming the protest, not just as a public display, but also as a private, personal choice to resist apathy, performance, and burnout. A work-hard-behind-the-scenes place to make the world better.

I don't have all the answers. I'm still figuring it out myself. But I do believe in asking better questions and not just the ones that look good on a T-shirt.

No performance. Just truth, curiosity, and maybe a little discomfort.

THE SELFIE AT THE PROTEST

Marching for Change to Posing for Clout

It used to be that if you believed in something, you showed up. You laced your shoes, grabbed a sign, and marched until your feet hurt or your voice gave out. Protests were loud, messy, sweaty acts of defiance. I am not talking about riots. Let's be clear. A riot involves violent and chaotic behavior that disrupts public order, often including vandalism, property damage, and physical aggression. I'm talking protests, which are public gatherings aimed at expressing disapproval or advocating for change, usually through peaceful methods such as speeches, marches, or signs. The smell of cardboard, Sharpie ink, and adrenaline. They are full-body experiences, not filtered moments.

The work behind the scenes? That's the hard part. When you are trying to fight for change, it isn't always in the picket signs, it's in the very difficult work that doesn't typically get the news coverage.

Now? Now protests and "work" have highlight reels.

We live in a time where resistance has a color palette, and every cause comes with a graphic pack. People ask what you're wearing to the protest like it's a launch party. Some of us wear our beliefs like accessories, a sticker here, a hashtag there, and perform activism in ways designed more to be seen than to be felt. There is a difference between showing up and showing off, and somehow, the line has gotten blurred.

The selfie at the protest is now its own genre. You've seen it: chin tilted at the perfect angle, sign visible but not too distracting, the crowd blurred artfully behind. There's usually a caption that reads something like, "So proud to stand

for what's right today. #JusticeFor_____"
It's not that the photo is fake. It's that the moment becomes about the image rather than the action. The bragging rather than the serving.

Let me state for the record, I'm not against selfies. I take them often. I'm not against people documenting what matters to them. I absolutely believe in using whatever platform you have to amplify truth. But I do think we need to talk about intent and purpose. About the performance of protest. About how, in the age of camera-ready everything, we are losing something raw and real about showing up for each other without needing to prove it to the internet or public common.

Part of the problem is that we are, by design, always watching and being watched. Social media makes spectators of all of us. Because we know we might be seen, we curate. Even the most spontaneous acts become opportunities to broadcast identity. We ask ourselves, "What will this say about me?" and adjust accordingly. Our activism gets run through the same filter we use for brunch photos.

There was a protest I watched one day a few years ago where I noticed more phones than signs. People weren't chanting so much as filming the chanting. One girl was doing full 360-degree slow-motion footage of herself walking with a fist raised, right there on the news. She looked powerful. Fierce. Cinematic. But she never said a word. Not a chant, not a cheer, not even a nod. When they interviewed her, she barely spoke about the actual issue she was protesting. She used the same common language we hear all the time. "I'm taking a stand," "I'm here in support," and "Justice can't wait." Yet, she never spoke about what she was standing for. I kept wondering who was she marching for? The cause or her followers?

The thing is, visibility is important. Documentation is powerful. The civil rights movement would not have had the same impact without the photos from Selma, or the footage of police brutality. Seeing is part of believing. Sharing can be part of spreading truth. However, at this current moment, it feels like the pendulum has swung too far. Now, many people aren't there to witness, they're there to be witnessed. Truth is relative, not definitive.

This has created a culture of protest as performance art. We hold signs with slogans we don't always understand. We join causes we haven't researched. We take up space without always thinking about who the space was originally meant for. Worst of all, we sometimes forget that action doesn't end when the livestream does. Real change requires follow-through. It requires silence, strategy, and sacrifice, none of which get good engagement. It's sweat and tears.

The rise of protest aesthetics has given birth to a new kind of social capital. Cloutivism, if you will. Where how you look while caring about something can matter more than whether you do anything about it. Let's be honest: it's tempting. It feels good to be seen doing something "right." But when our primary goal is to be perceived as "woke" or "on the right side," we stop asking harder questions. We trade substance for safety, boldness for branding.

I've done it, too. I've crafted the caption. I've watched the likes roll in and felt that warm buzz of affirmation. But then

I caught myself, realizing I spent more time editing a post than I did writing to my representative. That's when it hit me: I wasn't trying to change the world. I was trying to look like someone who might.

That realization was uncomfortable, but necessary. Because underneath all the posts and pledges is a truth that can't be styled: Activism is inconvenient. It requires risk. It asks us to prioritize others over ourselves. It's not cute. It doesn't always photograph well, and it sure doesn't need to trend to matter.

What we need is less performance in the public, more participation in the hard work. Less "proof" and more presence. Most of all, we need to remember that some of the most important work happens off-camera. It happens in conversations, in voting booths, in city council meetings, in messy personal group chats and sleepless nights. It happens when nobody is watching, and we do it anyway.

So, the next time you find yourself raising your phone before raising your voice, ask yourself: Who am I doing this for? Who benefits? What comes after the post? And if the only answer is "likes," then maybe it's time to log out and lean in.

Because the revolution might be televised, but the real work hardly ever is.

LIGHTS, CAMERA, CONSCIENCE

Surveillance Culture, Police Body Cams,
and the Panopticon Effect

It's a strange thing to be constantly watched. Stranger still is how quickly we've accepted it. Somewhere between convenience and compliance, we got comfortable with being on camera. Doorbells see us before our neighbors do. Phones record our lives better than we remember them. Public spaces come with disclaimers: "You are under video surveillance."

We don't blink anymore. The camera

is just part of the scenery now, like trees or streetlights or trash cans. We're aware of it, sure, but only in the way you're aware of wallpaper. Background. Static. Unavoidable. Unfortunately, in that quiet awareness, we've become something else: performers and followers.

We live in a world shaped by the panopticon. That old philosophical idea from Jeremy Bentham is a prison design where inmates could be watched at any time but never knew when. The result? They began to police themselves. That's where we are now. Only, we built the tower ourselves. We call it a phone. We call it a feed. We call it accountability, but sometimes it feels more like a trap we willingly walked into.

When body cameras were introduced as a solution to police brutality, the idea was simple, transparency would equal accountability. If officers knew they were being recorded, they'd behave better. If misconduct happened, there'd be proof. But years into widespread use, it's clear the reality is more complicated. Cameras catch violence, yes, but they don't always lead to justice. We've all seen the footage. Sometimes crystal-clear. Sometimes horrifying. Sometimes... ignored.

The problem isn't just whether something is recorded. It's who is watching. Who controls the narrative. Footage can be edited, suppressed, recontextualized. Even when it's shared uncut, people see what they want to see. Bias is a powerful lens. So, the question becomes, does being watched change behavior, or just shape how we defend it?

On the other side of the lens, civilians are watching, too. Filming. Streaming. Holding phones up like shields. There is power in documentation. There is undeniable bravery in capturing injustice and sharing it. But even here, surveillance becomes a double-edged sword. Activists have been tracked through their footage. Protesters have lost jobs for being caught on camera. Victims of violence have had their worst moments replayed endlessly online.

We're stuck in a cycle where visibility is both a weapon and a wound.

And then there's most of us, the everyday people caught somewhere in between. We know we're being watched, so we act accordingly. We pose. We edit. We rehearse our reactions. Think about it, when someone pulls out a phone, how many people adjust? How many suddenly "perform" empathy, outrage, concern, innocence? The camera isn't neutral. It changes the moment. It changes us.

Even politicians have learned to use this. They cry on cue. They visit sites of tragedy with a practiced look of solemnity, knowing the camera is rolling. They weaponize surveillance footage when it suits their agenda and discredits it when it doesn't. The presence of a camera used to imply truth. Now it implies spin.

Surveillance culture has seeped into our very sense of morality. We often behave not because it's right, but because it's trendy and someone might be filming. Our conscience is now tied to consequence. It's not "I shouldn't do this because it's wrong," but "I shouldn't do this because it might be filmed." That's a subtle but dangerous shift. One that means character is now circumstantial.

What happens when there is no camera? Do we still care? Will anyone believe it? If a person is harmed and it wasn't livestreamed, did it even happen in the eyes of the public? We've placed so much weight on what can be seen that we've forgotten to trust what can be known.

That's the haunting effect of being filmed at all times. It teaches us to trust only the visible. To seek proof for everything. In doing so, we lose the nuance of truth. The gray areas. The quiet injustices that don't scream into a lens. We give dangerous credibility to AI-generated content because we believe what we see. Only several years ago, people said, "I'd believe it if it were a video, but I can't trust a picture." Decades ago, it was, "Seeing is believing, and I'd believe it if there was a picture of it." Before that: witnesses.

There's a difference between accountability and exposure. What is truth and what can be "seen." The former is rooted in ethics. The latter in entertainment and perception. The line gets thinner every day.

I don't have a clean answer. Cameras can save lives. They can also ruin them. What I know is we need to be aware of the effect watching has on us. On how it shapes what we believe, how we behave, and who we choose to protect.

The lens can reveal or distort.

HASHTAG NATION

#Awareness vs. #Action

It started with a hashtag.
   Actually, it started with many.
   #MeToo
   #BlackLivesMatter
   #BringBackOurGirls
   #WhyIStayed
   #NeverAgain
   #YesAllWomen
   #Kony2012
   #FridaysForFuture
   #HeForShe

A phrase becomes a movement becomes a headline becomes a trend. In 280 characters or less, we condense trauma, urgency, outrage, and hope into a clickable phrase. The hashtags are meant to connect us. Sometimes, they do. But often, they simply signal that we care, or at least that we saw something worth caring about.

In 2014, #BlackLivesMatter took hold of the cultural conversation after the deaths of Michael Brown and Eric Garner. The hashtag became a rallying cry and a record. It helped local tragedies become national stories. Protesters in Ferguson were livestreaming clashes with police while journalists caught up. The tag outpaced the news cycle. For a moment, it felt like the internet was waking up.

Fast forward to 2020. George Floyd's murder was captured on camera, and within hours, #JusticeForGeorgeFloyd and #BlackLivesMatter were trending globally. The streets were filled with protesters. Social media feeds filled with black squares. The world was watching. Everyone, it seemed, had something to say.

But weeks later, the squares faded. The

statements slowed. The links to resources stopped circulating. What began as outrage settled into silence. Activism gave way to algorithm fatigue.

Still urgent, but it isn't trending anymore. That's what happens in the fatigue, many move quickly to the next trending hashtag.

The pattern isn't new. In 2014, after 276 Nigerian schoolgirls were kidnapped by Boko Haram, #BringBackOurGirls surged across platforms. The world demanded action. Years later, most of those girls are still missing, and the global attention has long moved on.

That's the tension at the heart of hashtag activism. It can elevate. It can amplify. *It can also flatten.* When we mistake awareness for action, we create a false sense of progress, which in turn can bring progress to a halt when the attention fades.

Part of the problem is social media moves fast. Nuance doesn't. Hashtags prioritize shareability, not complexity. So, we reduce causes to slogans. We shout over each other. We repeat the phrase until it loses meaning. When a new tragedy breaks, we abandon one tag for another, leaving movements unfinished in the digital graveyard of yesterday's discourse.

Hashtags are not inherently hollow. #MeToo, for instance, opened floodgates. It gave survivors a language, a space, and a signal. But even that movement, which began as a grassroots effort by Tarana Burke in 2006, got hijacked by mainstream attention cycles. It became more about headlines than healing. More about naming names than addressing systems.

The danger is that hashtags can be misused in the age of cancel culture, often hurting innocent people without proof in just one post. We post. We share. We feel involved. But posting isn't organizing. Sharing a graphic isn't policy work. Liking a tweet isn't community care. While all those things have their place, they're not enough and not always based in truth.

We have confused visibility with value. We think if something is trending, it must be true. Many people think that surely someone researched it already, or why else would it be trending. But hashtags can't replace truth and infrastructure. *They can't rewrite and enforce laws.* They can't fundraise, educate, or vote. They can start conversations, but they certainly can't finish them.

Some of the most effective movements never trend. Local organizers, mutual aid groups, and neighborhood coalitions often work quietly, steadily, with little recognition. No hashtags. No graphics. Just results.

It's not that hashtags are bad. They're tools. But like any tool, their power depends on how we use them. Are we amplifying voices, or just echoing slogans? Are we drawing attention to a cause, or to ourselves? Are we part of the solution, or just part of the noise? Are we spreading truth, or being an echo chamber of injustice?

The next time a hashtag surges, don't just repost it. Ask what it stands for. Who started it. Look for truth behind it. What it demands. Most importantly, ask what you can do after the hashtag fades to help make lasting change. Because hashtags may spark the fire, but they won't keep it burning.

Movements require more than momentum. They require work, action, infrastructure, and endurance.

THE INFLUENCE OF INFLUENCERS

When Advocacy Becomes Content

In June 2020, as protests swept the U.S. in the wake of George Floyd's murder, a video surfaced of a young woman, Fiona Moriarty-McLaughlin, in Los Angeles. She walked up to a boarded-up business, asked a construction worker if she could borrow his power drill to pose with it for a photo, then handed it back, smiled, and got into her car. Someone captured this, posted it stating she was never there to help. She was only there to be *seen* helping.

And it went viral.

This wasn't satire. It was influencer culture colliding with activism, gone wrong on so many levels. Did that one clip make her look like she was simply popularity posting? Yes, it did. Did the truth get the same amount of attention? It never does. Was it the smartest thing for her to do? No.

Truth is, she was writing a series of articles about George Floyd, the issues surrounding the incident, and curating content. Directly after the viral backlash, explaining the entire situation, which was proven by her many hours of footage she'd collected for the stories she was writing, corroborated by her employer and others who were helping her, did little good against that one post. The point is influencers have a place. A big one. They also have a responsibility. Unfortunately, many of them use their space to post current trendy issues, but some have a deeper purpose. Some want to effect change. They want to document it. They are in for the long haul.

With Fiona, the truth didn't matter, perception did. She was cancelled publicly and lost her internship. She has since regained her journalism career, been in several major news outlets, and I can only hope gained a better grasp of the responsibility she holds as a public figure, influencer, and journalist.

Do I agree that perception is reality? Yes and no. I agree that it is. That's human nature; we believe what we see. Even scripture says in 1 Thessalonians 5:22 to avoid the appearance of wrongdoing. Meaning, be mindful of how our actions might be perceived by others. Even if an action is not sinful in itself, if it could be easily misunderstood or lead others to think we are engaging in evil, it's best to avoid it. A lesson many of us have had to learn, Christian or not. However, persecuting someone based on a perceived sin isn't justice. It's gossip at its finest and can often land someone in a libel suit if it is untrue.

I remember when, once upon a time, being an "influencer" was about branding products: fashion, fitness, travel. Now, it's about branding values. Social justice has become a content category. Outrage is now a niche. Solidarity? Well, it's often just another aesthetic.

Influencer activism or *cloutivism,*

emerged when people realized that standing for something also drove traffic. Social engagement leads to media engagement leads to monetization. Soon after, the most important social movements of our time became backdrops for personal branding.

There's the influencer who used the caption "Stop Asian Hate" on a bikini selfie. The many who filmed a tearful Instagram story in front of a George Floyd mural. The ones who turned Gaza into a carousel post template, slides in blush pink and pale blue. With every new crisis, a flood of carefully curated posts follows, complete with personal anecdotes, affiliate links, and matching donation receipts.

The motivations vary. Some influencers mean well. Others see a trending topic and know how to capitalize. But in both cases, the same issue arises: who is the activism actually for?

I believe platforms matter. Influencers can use their reach for good. When done right, they can fundraise, raise awareness, amplify marginalized voices, and even a playing field. But more often than not, they center on themselves. The cause becomes content. The suffering becomes scenery. Meanwhile, people who influence for true change, or journalism, are getting lost in the noise.

Take the rise of "allyship reels." Short videos of influencers educating their followers, often starting with "Hey besties!" and ending with calls to "like and share if you care." The tone is breezy, the aesthetics are spotless. Somehow, we're talking about systemic injustice under ring lights and TikTok filters. While some people do learn from this content, others consume it like a trend, like, swipe, forget.

There's also the matter of who gets to be the face of advocacy. Influencers, who are often young and media-savvy tend to be praised for "raising awareness," even if they're late to the conversation. Meanwhile, activists who have been doing the work for years often get ignored, shadowbanned, or criticized for being "too angry." The algorithm favors the palatable over the radical, the well-lit over the well-informed.

In 2021, a viral trend called the "activist starter pack" made the rounds, mocking how some influencers treat protest culture as a fashion statement: combat boots, protest sign, iced matcha, black tote bag, aesthetic filter. *It was funny because it was true.* We have turned movements into moods.

This commodification of advocacy isn't new. In the '60s, civil rights leaders faced criticism for how their images were used in media. But what's different now is the sheer speed and scale of the performance and many times, the motivation behind it. With every phone comes a platform, with every platform comes the pressure to speak up, and with that pressure, a race to appear woke enough, but never so radical that you lose followers.

Even brands have adopted the influencer strategy. Companies tweet support for Pride Month while donating to anti-LGBTQ+ politicians. They sell "feminist" T-shirts made in overseas sweatshops. They issue statements about racial equity but keep their leadership teams strikingly homogenous. And influencers are often the middlemen, helping corporations look compassionate while staying profitable.

The result is an endless stream of curated concern. Well-meaning, often well-crafted, but ultimately surface-level. Because when advocacy becomes content, it's hard to tell whether someone is passionate or just posting what the algorithm likes.

So, where do we go from here?

We start by asking: Am I elevating the cause or centering myself? Is this about impact or optics? Have I listened before speaking? Shared resources before selfies? Researched the issues? Supported the people doing the work off-camera?

Influencers have power. But with that comes responsibility. Not just to speak up, but sometimes to step back. To pass the mic. To put their money, time, and reach where their captions are.

Because in the end, real change doesn't need a highlight reel. It needs humility.

THE CORPORATE CLAPBACK

When Pepsi Wants to Join the Revolution

In April 2017, Pepsi released a commercial featuring Kendall Jenner leaving a photo shoot to join a vague, upbeat protest in the streets. The climax? Jenner handing a police officer a can of Pepsi, which seemingly dissolves all tension and conflict in the crowd. Peace, love, and soda. The backlash was immediate. Critics slammed it for trivializing real protest movements, for using aesthetics of resistance to sell fizzy sugar water. Within 48 hours, Pepsi pulled the ad and issued an apology. But the damage was done. The brand had entered the arena of *"woke marketing"* and gotten totally burned.

This wasn't an isolated incident. It was a turning point.

Today, social justice is part of the branding playbook. Corporations know the language. They know the hashtags. They know the fonts to use when they release a statement. They roll out rainbow packaging in June. They tweet about "equity" in February. They promise to "do better" every time a scandal breaks. And for a few days, the internet nods, shares, and applauds. We love a brand with a conscience—until we realize it was just another campaign.

The term for this is woke-washing and it's when companies adopt the appearance of progressive values without backing them up with meaningful action. It's performative allyship, sanitized and scaled for consumer comfort. It's not new. But in the era of constant surveillance and social media outrage, it's reached a new level of polish.

Consider how many brands posted black squares during #BlackOutTuesday in 2020. From fast food chains to luxury fashion houses, the stream of solidarity was endless. But behind the scenes? Many of those same companies had no plans for policy change, had never donated to racial justice organizations.

Or look at Pride Month. Every June, companies transform their logos into rainbows. They release collections of rainbow sneakers, rainbow fries, rainbow vodka. And yet, some of those same companies sell rainbow merchandise made in factories in countries where LGBTQ+ rights are non-existent.

It's capitalism dressed in a protest pin.

In 2018, Nike launched its now-famous ad campaign featuring Colin Kaepernick, with the slogan "Believe in something. Even if it means sacrificing everything." The ad went viral. People praised Nike for taking a stand. Others burned their sneakers. All the while, behind the scenes, Nike made billions in brand value. They bet on controversy and won. Was it brave, or just brilliant marketing?

That's the dilemma. Many brands don't have morals. They have market research. When they "take a stand," it's usually because the data says it's safe for their consumer. Not necessarily because they believe it. Their primary goal is loyalty. Loyalty that translates into sales. In that sense, outrage is just another currency.

Some companies have even flipped their social media strategies to become part of the clapback culture. Wendy's, for example, gained massive online attention with its sassy, unfiltered Twitter persona, taking jabs at other brands, joking about politics, and leaning into chaos. It worked. Other brands followed suit, hoping to appear edgy and aware. But at what point does the snark become a distraction from real accountability?

This kind of branding co-opts the language of movements. It packages protest into palatable chunks. It trains us to expect change in the form of a statement or a campaign, rather than legislation or labor reform. And because it looks like progress, we sometimes forget to demand the real thing.

The irony? Many of these same companies resist actual change within. They underpay workers and often avoid unionization efforts wanted by employees. Some issue diversity reports but rarely appoint diverse leadership. They want the look of justice without the cost. Be

Jereme Silltech

clear, I'm not saying all companies should push to hire diverse leadership if the most qualified applicants available aren't diverse. I'm saying don't optic a belief you don't believe in. If they believed in diverse leadership, they would hire a headhunter to seek out qualified diversity.

It's not wrong to want brands to care. But caring costs something, and when a brand's values change with the quarterly forecast, we should be cautious about giving them too much credit.

So how do we tell the difference between genuine allyship and a PR stunt?

Look at consistency, and like any good investigation, look at motive. Review their track record. Where the money goes. Who's in leadership. What policies they support behind the scenes. And whether their so-called values show up when the cameras aren't rolling.

We shouldn't expect companies to lead revolutions. We also shouldn't let them borrow the language of revolution to sell leggings. Because real change doesn't come in a limited-edition box. It comes from sacrifice and sustained action.

It comes from freedom and equity. Value and validity.

Many people have lost everything because they stood for something. They didn't stand for everything trendy. They didn't monetize, they prioritized. They may have lost their lives for what they believed, because they backed up what they believed with everything they owned.

That's something no campaign slogan can fake.

DENIM, DISCOMFORT, AND DOUBLE STANDARDS

When Outrage Outpaces Understanding

In July 2025, American Eagle released a commercial featuring actress Sydney Sweeney, a starlet, Gen Z icon who is no stranger to cultural controversy. In the ad, she dances, laughs, and leans in suggestively wearing a pair of jeans, while a soft voiceover lists her "genes." It was playful. Edgy. It sparked outrage almost instantly.

Critics blasted the commercial for being too sexual, too shallow, too white, too beautiful. Some said it glamorized domestic violence. Others argued that focusing on Sweeney's "genes" while she flaunted her jeans was tone-deaf. A few claimed the entire message was confusing.

What exactly was American Eagle trying to say?

Here's what they were saying, and what many missed: 100% of the proceeds from the jeans mentioned in the ad are being donated to the Crisis Text Line, a nonprofit that provides mental health support and crisis intervention, including help for people experiencing domestic abuse. But unless you dug deeper, or waited until the end screen of the ad, you may not have known that. Most didn't. Most reacted to the optics.

That's the world we live in now. An ad drops. Screenshots circulate. TikToks analyze the first five seconds. Twitter threads explode with hot takes. Few ask follow-up questions. Fewer still ask what the impact actually is.

Let me talk about the controversy first.

The criticism that the ad is too sexual to support a campaign against domestic abuse is not just misleading, it's harmful. Domestic abuse doesn't happen because a woman is attractive. It doesn't happen because of tight jeans, exposed skin, or flirtatious laughter. It happens because of power, control, trauma, and violence. Blaming the way a woman looks or dances is dangerously close to the logic used to excuse abusers in the past. It has been used many times to explain why men rape, degrade, and even kill women. It's the same logic that says, "Well, what was she wearing?" only now it's dressed in progressive outrage.

Second, the attack on Sweeney herself, especially because she is white, blonde, and blue-eyed, reveals something even more troubling. Some posts framed her casting as a symbol of exclusion. As if her very existence somehow invalidates the cause. As if fighting for marginalized voices requires silencing others. As if beauty, or whiteness, automatically makes someone complicit in oppression.

That's not justice. That's a new and disturbing kind of gatekeeping.

Fighting for equality means fighting for everyone's safety and dignity, not just those who fit a certain profile of struggle. Domestic abuse doesn't discriminate by race, hair color, or eye shape, and neither should compassion and change.

Was the ad perfectly executed? Arguably not. It could have communicated the cause more clearly. It could have made the donation aspect more prominent. But what it actually did, quietly and meaningfully, was something that far too few brands do: put its money where its mouth is. Donating all profits from a product to a real, active mental health and domestic abuse organization. No fine print. No partial percentages. No conditions. Just action. It also caused a conversation like this. Who is allowed to be a voice? Who is allowed to have space to speak? Can equality be real if only certain people are "allowed."

Some people have speculated that American Eagle knew this would spark backlash. That the brand anticipated the noise and used the tension between sex appeal and activism to stir the pot. Maybe. But if they did, they also used that attention to point toward something real. They turned controversy into contribution, and in a world where most brands just post pastel-colored infographics or stir the pot for profit and move on, that matters.

Meanwhile, many of the loudest critics

were using their own platforms to do... what, exactly? Post hot takes? Go viral? Get clout for calling something out? Cameras are powerful tools, but they can't always tell the whole story. In this case, they have, at least, distorted it. At most, rolled back victim's advocacy.

Here's a bigger irony: the very people outraged about the optics are often guilty of the same thing they're condemning and focusing on appearance over substance. Sydney Sweeney's beauty and whiteness became the enemy, not because she did something harmful, but because her face didn't match someone's idea of what activism should look like.

When we start picking apart who is allowed to speak out, who is allowed to help, and who is allowed to be featured in a campaign for a cause that affects everyone, or who is qualified to be a part of change, we're not pushing for progress. We're reinforcing a new kind of purity politics, one where intention and impact are irrelevant unless they look exactly how we want them to.

This moment was a mirror: for branding, for outrage culture, and for all of us. Because in the midst of all the noise, a brand tried to give away 100% of its profits for something good, and somehow, that got lost.

Did their stocks soar? Yes. Did they sell other jeans that weren't a part of the campaign? Yes. Did they expect the backlash? I can only guess in our current culture they did. Was there a worry that this would not go over well, possibly negatively backfire? Again, in our current culture, I can only speculate that they did. However, what we *know* they did was raise enormous amounts of funds to further crisis help for others and sparked a new relevant conversation that has long been needed.

Maybe it's time we stop trying to "catch" each other being imperfect and start noticing who's actually trying to help. Maybe it's time we give less attention to what makes us angry, and more to what creates positive change for all. Maybe we stop filming our outrage and start funding some solutions.

Because jeans don't cause abuse. Beauty doesn't cause abuse.

Ignoring the deeper truth while chasing the perfect optics?

That does.

THE AUTHORITY DECLINE

Trading Law for Misjustice

Swing one way or the other in a conversation these days, depending on present company, and it might go very, very badly. When people wager everything on their beliefs, but they are in a place of authority or represent a certain group of people, it gets hairy.

As prime examples, in recent years, a growing number of judges and prosecutors have been accused of trading justice for activism, using their courtrooms as stages for political theater rather than sanctuaries for impartial law. Instead of interpreting statutes through the lens of precedent and constitutional balance, some legal officials now appear more interested in advancing social agendas, often with the cameras rolling. Progressive district attorneys in cities like San Francisco and Philadelphia, for example, have declined to prosecute entire categories of crimes, such as certain thefts and drug offenses, not based on changes to the law but on personal ideology. This has led to public frustration as repeat offenders walk free, eroding public trust in the system meant to protect them.

On the judicial side, judges have made headlines for issuing rulings that appear more rooted in political signaling than in the rule of law, such as blocking laws not based on constitutional grounds but due to perceived "moral opposition." In some high-profile cases, judges have even used their platforms to make sweeping, emotionally charged statements to the press, signaling allegiance to causes rather than legal clarity. While personal conviction is part of every human decision, when justice becomes a performance for media optics, the line between law and ideology blurs dangerously, threatening the foundational principle that all are equal under the law, not under political preference.

Several high-profile prosecutors and judges have come under fire for overriding the law in favor of their own personal or political beliefs, often at the expense of public safety and the justice system's integrity. Now, many people would agree that they can have their freedom of speech, their freedom of beliefs, and their freedom of principles, and I agree, they can. However, they cannot inject them into a job that requires them to literally override their own beliefs to meet out justice with honor.

Former San Francisco District Attorney Chesa Boudin refused to prosecute crimes like shoplifting, drug offenses, and prostitution, actions rooted more in progressive activism than in legal precedent. His decisions were followed by a sharp rise in repeat offenses, prompting a voter-led recall in 2022. Similarly, Cook County State's Attorney Kim Foxx faced national outrage after dropping all charges against actor Jussie Smollett despite strong evidence he staged a hate crime. Though she claimed to have recused herself, Foxx remained involved in the case, leading to an independent investigation and a scathing court rebuke that labeled her office's actions "a major failure of justice." In Los Angeles, District Attorney George Gascón implemented sweeping reforms eliminating cash bail, the death penalty, and sentencing enhancements, even for violent crimes, policies so extreme that his own prosecutors sued him for forcing them to violate California law and ignore victims' rights. Meanwhile, Philadelphia District Attorney Larry Krasner was accused of allowing violent repeat offenders to walk free through lenient plea deals and refusal to prosecute, contributing to a crime surge and culminating in his impeachment by the Pennsylvania House.

Judges, too, have inserted ideology into their rulings. Massachusetts Judge Shelley Richmond Joseph allegedly helped an undocumented immigrant evade ICE by letting him slip out a courthouse back door, leading to federal obstruction charges and turning her case into a national symbol of judicial defiance against immigration enforcement. Even though federal obstruction of justice charges against Joseph were dropped in 2022 after she agreed to refer herself to the Commission on Judicial Conduct, they concluded in 2024 that Joseph "engaged in willful judicial misconduct that brought the judicial office into disrepute, as well as conduct prejudicial to the administration of justice and unbecoming a judicial officer." In California, Judge Aaron Persky sparked outrage after sentencing Stanford student Brock Turner to just six months for sexual assault, citing concern for the perpetrator's future rather than justice for the victim. The public viewed this as a case of racial and class-based favoritism, resulting in Persky's recall, the first in California in nearly a century. Lastly, Judge Emmet Sullivan of the U.S. District Court for D.C. ignited controversy when he refused to dismiss charges against Michael Flynn, despite the Department of Justice dropping the case. Many legal experts criticized him for overstepping his role as a judge and venturing into prosecutorial territory, leading to intervention from a higher court. Collectively, these cases reflect a troubling pattern: legal authorities abandoning neutrality to promote personal causes, eroding public trust in a system meant to function above politics.

These cases underscore a troubling trend, instead of quietly and impartially interpreting the law, some legal officials appear more focused on shaping narratives, gaining media attention, or aligning with activist causes, transforming the courtroom from a place of objective justice into a platform for personal or political expression. Because the law is essential for preserving a stable and fair society. It creates structure, safeguards individual rights, and ensures accountability. Additionally, the law offers a foundation for resolving conflicts, advancing social development, and reinforcing moral and ethical principles. So if laws ensure that individuals, organizations, and governments are held accountable for their actions, preventing corruption and abuse of power, how is it that people in power think they are able to circumvent it?

These examples demonstrate how individual actors within the justice system can undermine public confidence by allowing politics, media pressure,

Jereme Silltech

or personal beliefs to override legal obligations and neutral enforcement.

THE ACTIVIST ALGORITHM

The Cause That Gets Clicks Wins

Unless you were actively looking for updates about protesters risking their lives to resist military control in 2021, where dozens were killed in the streets, you probably didn't hear much about Myanmar. I wouldn't have either if my husband hadn't told me about it because it never truly "trended." It wasn't looped on the news every hour, and no one seemed to care that much about it. Meanwhile, a celebrity breakup and a viral dance challenge dominated my feed for days.

It's not that we don't care, it's that the algorithm didn't.

This is the quiet power of the algorithm. It decides what we see, what we share, what gets amplified, and what gets buried. And when it comes to activism, that power shapes what causes rise to public consciousness, and which ones disappear before they even begin.

Social media platforms were once praised for democratizing information. Anyone could speak. Anyone could go viral. While that's technically still true, the rules have changed. Content that provokes outrage, simplifies complexity, or aligns with already-popular narratives rise to the top. Movements that are difficult, nuanced, or uncomfortable for the current culture often struggle to stay visible. If you look a certain way, and do not align with the current trend, you are expected to move out of the way.

In the summer of 2020, posts about racial justice surged. Algorithms pushed #BlackLivesMatter content to the top of every feed. But as the months passed, engagement waned. Not because the cause became less important, but because the algorithm rewarded novelty. Once the initial wave of posts slowed, which they always do, platforms shifted attention to more profitable content. TikTok dances. Sponsored content. Branded challenges.

The thing is activism isn't profitable. Outrage is. So, the algorithm promotes posts that generate strong emotional reactions—anger, fear, indignation. Activism competes with entertainment. Causes must be condensed into catchy visuals, ten-second videos, or digestible carousels. The deeper, harder parts, the history, the policy, the work, get lost in the scroll.

We saw this during the pandemic. As many people fell into depression, others were posting more Christian content than ever. Soon, people who had posted Christian content were complaining that their posts were glitching or vanishing altogether. The social media platform later claimed it was a technical bug. Whether it was or wasn't, it sparked a conversation about who controls the narrative, and how quickly information can be filtered, flagged, or vanished entirely by systems we don't understand.

Algorithms on platforms like TikTok have faced criticism for suppressing content from marginalized creators. Many non-trending advocates have all reported lower visibility—even when their content follows the rules. The systems, they argue, weren't built for them, and when they speak out, they're often accused of being too "aggressive," "negative," or "off-brand."

This creates a chilling effect. To be seen, activists either feel pressure to soften their tone, brighten their visuals, and package their message in a way that's "safe" for wide consumption or go full blast, no stop, unfiltered anger. Why? Engagement, of course. It's all in the algorithm.

The activist algorithm rewards the palatable and the provocative. It nudges us toward performative engagement, without requiring much truth or depth. It tells us that caring is about visibility, not commitment. It conditions us to expect change to be immediate, packaged, and emotionally satisfying, whether that be feel-good or rage.

But real change isn't always viral. It's slow. It's messy. It doesn't come with likes or anger emoji's.

The challenge is resisting the pressure

to "trend" our values. Just because a post performs well doesn't mean it's right. Just because a movement is invisible online doesn't mean it's not working offline. Algorithms are designed to reflect our engagement, not our ethics.

We have to take back some control. That means following organizers directly. Seeking out independent media. Remembering that our feeds are curated, not comprehensive.

The algorithm is powerful, but it's not neutral. If we continue to let it guide our sense of justice, we'll miss the movements that matter most.

THE BURNOUT GENERATION

Fighting for Everything,
Standing for Nothing

In the weeks following a 2020 uprisings, a popular meme made the rounds on Instagram: "This is not a moment, it's a movement." The intention was noble, to remind people that justice requires long-term commitment. But as the news cycle moved on and social media feeds filled back up with lifestyle content and brand collabs, it became clear: for many, it was a moment... and that moment had passed.

Burnout is not just a side effect of

activism today. It's baked into the system. The sheer velocity of causes, tragedies, and calls to action has turned caring into a full-time job. One week, you're organizing a fundraiser. The next, you're posting a thread about climate disasters. Then a school shooting. Then another. Then a leaked Supreme Court decision. Then a police killing. Then a natural disaster. Then a war. The carousel never stops. Toppled with all the #weddingbliss and #newbaby posts, our heads are constantly spinning in and out of emotional draws.

"Social media fatigue" is a term often used to describe the constant shifts we experience in emotional tone, from positive to negative, while scrolling through social media. The ups and downs cause us to not only become fatigued emotionally, but physically it takes a major toll on our bodies. It causes us to experience a form of compassion fatigue also. In a group setting it's gotten so bad that one friend can share that they are going through a tragedy, and another still feel it's okay to share their great news of the day, barely missing a pause in conversation.

The term "compassion fatigue" was first used in the 1990s to describe the emotional strain experienced by nurses and first responders. Now it describes an entire generation trying to keep up with a world on fire. Activism fatigue. Outrage fatigue. Empathy overload. Emotional overload. We're not just burned out from doing too much. We're burned out from feeling too much and not knowing what to do with it.

A 2021 study by the American Psychological Association found that nearly sixty percent of Americans felt "overwhelmed by the number of issues facing the world." Many reported feeling hopeless, anxious, and numb. Here's the catch: the people who care the most are often the most exhausted. The people trying to keep everyone informed, mobilized, and engaged are the ones collapsing behind closed doors.

In 2018, activist Brittany Packnett Cunningham tweeted, "You're not obligated to set yourself on fire to keep others warm." It resonated widely because even among organizers, there's an unspoken expectation to always be on. Always have a take. Always post. Always respond. If you stop, even to rest, you risk being labeled as disengaged or indifferent.

Worse, you lose your algorithm advantage.

Social media accelerates the burnout cycle. Algorithms reward urgency. The more you post, the more you stay visible. The more visible you are, the more people expect of you. It's a loop: speak up, go viral, get overwhelmed, disappear, come back, repeat. And it's not just public figures, everyday people feel it too. The pressure to stay informed, react immediately, and present a curated form of concern becomes a quiet, constant drain.

This burnout is not a personal failure. It's a systemic issue.

We're not equipped to handle such a volume of information, whether good or bad. The human brain isn't wired to carry the pain, and all the ups and downs of the world in our back pocket. But our phones demand it. Every scroll brings more grief, more rage, more helplessness. Cute puppy on one screen, to a starving, abandoned one on the next.

During the height of the pandemic, mutual aid groups became lifelines for communities left behind by government systems. They coordinated food, rent relief, medical supplies. But by late 2021, many of those groups had disbanded, not because the need had vanished, but because the volunteers were exhausted. Burnout isn't just emotional. It dismantles entire movements.

Some organizers have started to speak openly about stepping back. They've deleted apps. Taken sabbaticals. Moved to slower models of engagement. This isn't apathy, it's strategy. Rest is resistance. Boundaries are survival.

There's power in pacing ourselves. There's wisdom in stepping back so we can come back stronger. *Activism that depends on constant crisis is not sustainable.* Movements need longevity. Longevity requires rest, reflection, and a realistic sense of our limits.

The guilt we carry for resting is a tool of oppression. The urgency we feel is real, but urgency without direction becomes noise, and noise is not the same as movement.

You are not a news ticker. You are not a spokesperson for every injustice. You are a person... and people need rest.

The goal is not to be constantly engaged; it's to be consistently committed, and that means knowing when to log off, recharge, and return with clarity.

Because a burned-out voice can't call for change.

And a burned-out heart can't hold hope.

THE SILENCE OF THE REAL

What We've Lost in the Noise

Many stories barely registered in the national conversation, because slow activism rarely does.

We live in a culture that rewards the loud, the fast, the reactive. But some of the most important change is quiet. It happens in community meetings, local hearings, and long, un-Instagrammable conversations. It happens in organizing spreadsheets, or on phone trees. The kind of work that doesn't trend, doesn't photograph well, and doesn't generate clicks.

In 2019, the story of the Detroit Water Shutoffs surfaced in local reporting: tens of thousands of residents had their water turned off due to unpaid bills. Families were forced to choose between groceries and plumbing. National media outlets barely noticed. But grassroots organizers, like We the People of Detroit, had been working on the issue for years. Not for clout. For survival.

Did anyone really expect a company that has the goal of making money to care if they shut off electricity to people who didn't pay for their services? Yes, the activists that wanted a stage.

But the true issue wasn't about the company doing their job, it was about the people who needed help. The activists who stepped in didn't blame the company, they helped the people. That's what the base of activism is. True activism is marked by helping.

The silence around real, complex stories isn't an accident. It's a byproduct of a media and platform economy driven by speed and virality. Long-form journalism has shrunk. Local newsrooms are underfunded. Deep investigations are buried beneath trending tags. Yet, those slow stories are the ones that tell us who we really are. Who the true activists really are. The real stories that create real, direct results *for people*, not just results online.

We've been trained to think that change looks like a mic drop. A speech that goes viral. A headline that breaks the internet. However, in truth, change often looks like a coalition budget meeting at 9 a.m. on a Tuesday. It looks like someone staying after a protest to clean up. Like a librarian stocking books on tenant rights. Like someone sitting across from their city council rep with a binder full of data and a calm voice full of fire.

These stories aren't sexy. They aren't shareable. Still, they're the foundation. Without them, nothing scalable survives.

Remember the Montgomery Bus Boycott? It lasted over a year. Most people today recall the story as a single heroic act by Rosa Parks, but it was actually a deeply strategic, slow-burn effort led by women organizers, church leaders, and local networks. They met. They planned. They sacrificed. No tweets. No TikToks. Just unwavering, offline commitment.

The same goes for the ACT UP movement

during the AIDS crisis in the 1980s. Yes, they staged dramatic die-ins and protests, but much of the real progress came from years of policy research, lobbying, and behind-the-scenes pressure on drug companies and lawmakers. The camera captured the drama. But the change was born in the rooms no one filmed.

Today, we risk forgetting those models. We've mistaken volume for value. Screaming and streaming for stepping up (or sometimes sitting down). We assume what's visible is what's vital. But the real work often happens in silence. And it's precisely that silence that gives it staying power.

We need to make peace with being uncelebrated. To understand that some work will not be witnessed and that doesn't make it any less worthy. There's a kind of sacredness in the quiet labor of change. A humility in doing what matters even when no one is watching.

Even those doing the quiet work feel pressure to perform. To post their progress. To prove their impact. The digital world whispers constantly: "If you didn't share it, did it even happen?"

Yes. Yes, it did.

Sometimes, the most radical act is refusing to document it.

None of this is to say that media is the enemy. Documentation matters. So does storytelling. But not everything should be content. Not every win needs a reel. Some victories are personal and sacred. Some work is best done in the shadows, not because it's secret, but because it's strong enough to not need spotlight to get the work done.

So let's not forget the power of the unfilmed.

The emails sent.

The community fridges stocked.

The petitions read line by line.

The quiet volunteers who keep showing up.

The policy changes.

In a world full of constant, unrelenting noise, silence isn't apathy. Sometimes, it's the deepest form of commitment.

BEYOND THE OPTICS

Reclaiming Protest and Participation

For too long now, we've been trained to think of activism as a spectacle. Something to witness, applaud, share. While that visibility has power, it can't be the end goal. We must unlearn the belief that being seen is the same thing as being effective. The real question is: what happens after the photo?

It's not just a single protest or viral image. It's the days of walking, organizing carpools, and demanding legal change. It's lawyers, teachers, and grandmothers working together. No one waiting for a news crew to show up to start the work.

When Standing Rock protestors set up camp in 2016 to resist the Dakota Access Pipeline, it began as a prayer circle and became an international movement. Much of the early resistance wasn't televised. It was organized through tribal elders, community meetings, and intergenerational planning. What the cameras eventually captured was just a fraction of the labor and spirit already happening.

To move beyond optics, we need to return to substance and strategy. That means digging deeper than headlines and hashtags. It means understanding the systems we're up against, how city councils vote, how school boards operate, how policies are written and rewritten. It means not just showing up to the march, but showing up to the meeting after. And the meeting after that.

It also means making space for many forms of participation. Not everyone can protest in the streets. Some people write letters. Some cook meals for organizers. Some translate flyers. Some provide childcare. Every act matters. Every role counts. We've placed too much emphasis on the most visible types of activism and not enough on the quiet, essential work behind the scenes.

Beyond optics, activism is uncomfortable. It's slow. It's full of setbacks. It's also where real change lives. It's where people learn to disagree and still collaborate. Where they challenge their own biases, not just other people's. Where they commit to the long haul, not just the highlight.

Moving beyond optics also means embracing messiness. Real organizing doesn't always look organized. It means miscommunication, late nights, lost sleep, and group texts that go nowhere. It also means breakthroughs, relationships, transformation. The work isn't polished—but it's real.

To reclaim protest and participation, we have to stop asking, "Will this look good?" and start asking, "Will this work?" We have to prioritize outcomes over aesthetics, equity over engagement, and people over platforms.

You don't have to be an expert to start. You just have to start. Find one issue in your community. Show up. Ask questions.

Offer help. Make mistakes. Keep going.

Because beyond the optics, there's a movement waiting for you. Not one that needs your perfection, but your persistence.

TRUTH OVER OPTICS

A Personal Manifesto
for Conscious Resistance

This chapter isn't a guide. It's a permission slip.

To stop performing. Stop proving. Step back from the spotlight. Resist in ways that aren't always seen, shared, or shaped for applause. Be committed even when it's quiet, slow, and entirely offline.

I've spent too much time worrying if I'm doing it "right." If I'm posting enough, learning enough, responding fast enough, staying relevant, sounding smart, showing up, standing up, speaking out. Every time I failed to meet that impossible bar.

Conscious resistance means choosing how and when you engage, not letting the machine dictate it. It means unfollowing pressure, not people. It means being brave enough to go against the grain of engagement culture and trust that the real work might not get you followers, but it will reclaim your voice.

We've seen this modeled by people who choose truth over optics every day.

In 2022, a small group of librarians in Llano County, Texas, refused to comply with orders to remove books from shelves that centered LGBTQ+ characters and racial justice topics. They didn't go viral. They didn't trend. They just said no. They lost their jobs, but they didn't lose their clarity.

That same year, several Christian groups across the country started the "parental rights" movement, who actively sought to expand parental control over what is taught in schools, including topics related to sexual orientation and gender identity. This wasn't directly in opposition to the librarians in Llano County, it was in agreement with their own faith. It wasn't flashy and didn't make it on the news loops.

I applaud both for standing up for what they believe in. It's our right in this country to do so.

There's nothing wrong with visibility, but it's not the only metric. There's nothing wrong with sharing, but it's not the only kind of solidarity. We need to remember what it means to stand for something without needing to be seen doing it.

You can protest by refusing to repost. You can resist by slowing down. You can learn by researching. You can fight back by logging off. You can unlearn, rewire, and act from a deeper place than panic. That's not passivity. That's power.

If I stop showing up in the way the feed demands. If I don't have a hot take on every injustice. If I take time to learn quietly. If I mourn in private. If I resist the urge to brand my beliefs. If I refuse to make pain performative. If I prioritize depth over delivery. If I choose to grow out of view. It's okay, because I am still working on the things I believe in. I haven't stopped working. I've stopped seeking approval for it.

Because the future isn't found in the

comments. It's found in the connections we protect, the truths we live, and the justice we build when no one's watching.

If you're still here, you were not here reading for the trend, anyway.

NOTE FROM THE AUTHOR

Working for Lasting Impact

This book was born from a deep ache and a quiet hope. I wrote it not because I have it all figured out, but because I don't. Like many of you, I've been overwhelmed. Disillusioned. Exhausted by the pace of online expectations and the pressure to always "show up" in public ways. This book is my way of slowing down, digging deeper, and learning.

If any part of this resonated with you, if it gave you language, or relief, or something to wrestle with, I'm grateful.

If you don't agree with every page, I'm grateful for that too. Disagreement means you're thinking on your own, and that's the point.

ABOUT THE AUTHOR

Jereme Silltech writes bold, thought-provoking nonfiction that invites readers to step out of performative culture and into deeper truth. With a sharp eye for modern contradictions and a heart grounded in her Christian faith, she tackles everything from identity and belief to the subtle lies of the culture-common narrative. Known for a voice that's equal parts grace and grit, Jereme calls readers to real freedom, the kind that can't be hashtagged, branded, or bought.

Whether challenging cultural norms with unflinching determination, or unpacking Scripture for everyday life Jereme writes for those hungry to live with purpose, conviction, and courage in a culture-common world that only wants followers.

References

CDC: Intimate Partner Violence Fast Facts
https://www.cdc.gov/violenceprevention/intimatepartnerviolence/fastfact.html

CDC: National Intimate Partner and Sexual Violence Survey (NISVS)
https://www.cdc.gov/violenceprevention/pdf/nisvs-statereportbook.pdf

CDC: 2015 Data Brief
https://www.cdc.gov/violenceprevention/pdf/2015data-brief508.pdf

Break the Cycle: Domestic Violence Statistics
https://www.breakthecycle.org/domestic-violence-statistics

The Hotline: Domestic Violence Statistics
https://www.thehotline.org/stakeholders/domestic-violence-statistics/

Dolan + Zimmerman LLP: Domestic Violence Statistics

https://www.dolanzimmerman.com/domestic-violence-statistics/

USA Today: Fiona Moriarty-McLaughlin Opinion Piece

https://www.usatoday.com/story/opinion/2020/06/24/black-lives-matter-viral-video-woman-plywood-california-column/3236205001/

Pepsi Ad Backlash (2017 Coverage) – The Guardian

https://www.theguardian.com/media/2017/apr/05/pepsi-ad-kendall-jenner-backlash-protests

Nike Kaepernick Campaign: Forbes Analysis

https://www.forbes.com/sites/kurtbadenhausen/2018/09/24/nikes-kaepernick-ad-campaign-is-driving-sales-and-traffic/

Blackout Tuesday Brand Response Summary

https://www.vox.com/2020/6/2/21278131/blackout-tuesday-instagram-explained-george-floyd

Chesa Boudin Recall – New York Times

https://www.nytimes.com/2022/06/08/us/chesa-boudin-recall.html

Kim Foxx & Jussie Smollett Case – NPR
https://www.npr.org/2021/12/08/1062558704/jussie-smollett-trial-explained

George Gascón Controversy – Los Angeles Times
https://www.latimes.com/california/story/2021-02-22/da-gascon-sued-by-own-prosecutors-over-policy-changes

Larry Krasner Impeachment – Associated Press
https://apnews.com/article/pennsylvania-larry-krasner-impeachment-4b56054b9737cf42bc6fd66ea0c88d86

Shelley Richmond Joseph Case – NPR
https://www.npr.org/2022/09/23/1124549834/judge-shelley-richmond-joseph-federal-case-dismissed

Judge Aaron Persky Recall – CNN
https://www.cnn.com/2018/06/06/us/aaron-persky-recall-brock-turner/index.html

Judge Emmet Sullivan / Michael Flynn Case – Politico
https://www.politico.com/news/2020/05/21/judge-michael-flynn-case-274188

Sydney Sweeney / American Eagle Backlash – The Guardian
https://www.theguardian.com/us-news/2025/jul/29/american-eagle-sydney-sweeney-jeans-ad

American Eagle Donating 100% of Proceeds – Pedestrian TV

https://www.pedestrian.tv/entertainment/sydney-sweeney-american-eagle-response/

TikTok Algorithm & Marginalized Creators – MIT Technology Review

https://www.technologyreview.com/2020/07/08/1004540/tiktok-algorithm-black-creators-marginalized-content-suppression/

APA Stress Study 2021

https://www.apa.org/news/press/releases/stress/2021/march-2021-survey.pdf

We the People of Detroit – Grassroots Activism

https://www.wethepeopleofdetroit.com/

Crisis Text Line Official Site

https://www.crisistextline.org/

www.ingramcontent.com/pod-product-compliance
Lightning Source LLC
Chambersburg PA
CBHW071341290326
41933CB00040B/1911